FOOTBA GROUNDS IN LONDON

from the air

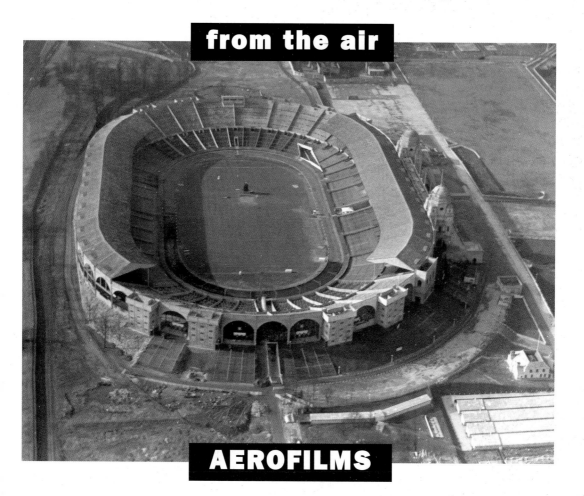

AEROFILMS

Ian Allan PUBLISHING

▲ Watford
13 June 1969
(A196007; see pp88-93)

First published 2006

ISBN (10) 0 7110 3186 X
ISBN (13) 978 0 7110 3186 9

Published by Ian Allan Publishing

an imprint of Ian Allan Publishing Ltd, Hersham, Surrey KT12 4RG.

Printed by Ian Allan Printing Ltd, Hersham, Surrey KT12 4RG.

Code: 0610/C

Visit the Ian Allan Publishing website at:
www.ianallanpublishing.com

Title Page
Wembley
10 February 1928
(20340; see pp106-114)

Front cover
Arsenal
25 May 2006
(700184; see pp6-17)

Back cover, top
Arsenal
23 March 1928
(25837; see pp6-17)

Back cover, bottom
Wembley
7 May 1955
(A58472; see pp106-114)

Introduction   4

League Clubs:

Wembley

Non-League Clubs:

Tottenham Hotspur
10 September 1966
during a Spurs and Manchester United game
(A167143; see pp80-87)

The Greater London area currently possesses no fewer than 13 Premier or Football League teams as well as myriad semi-professional, amateur and other football clubs competing in the non-league pyramid. Irrespective of the size of the club, there is one constant: the need for somewhere to play. Whilst the facilities and scale may differ between the grounds in the professional game and those in the non-league pyramid, the basic requirements remain the same: the provision of a playing surface, facilities for the players and an environment in which spectators can watch the match in safety.

Although the origins of many clubs and the grounds that they occupy predate World War 1, the massive expansion in the facilities offered at football grounds was very much a product of the interwar years. It was during this period that, for example, Wembley Stadium was built as were the now-listed East and West stands at Arsenal's Highbury ground.

From the immediate post-World War 1 years the Aerofilms company has been recording the changing landscape of the British Isles. Inevitably, during this process, football grounds have been recorded, either deliberately or by accident, and through the unique archive that the Aerofilms company has built up over a near 90-year period it is possible to trace the development of many of the great football grounds. The coverage over the past 14 years has been fostered by the annual

publication of *Aerofilms Guide: Football Grounds*, which has faithfully recorded the phenomenal development of Premier and Football League clubs since the early 1990s. In many respects, in terms of the rapidly changing face of football – not just in London but across the country – the past decade has witnessed arguably the fastest changes to football grounds than in any period in the game's history other than during the years immediately after World War 1.

Inevitably, the coverage of grounds is not wholly comprehensive; in particular the non-league scene in London has not been recorded as widely as the major league grounds. What is possible, however, through the Aerofilms' archive is to trace the development of all of London's league grounds and Wembley in some detail and also provide

Fulham
1949
(A22168/49; see pp50–55)

a selection of non-league grounds. The latter, unfortunately, can be no more than a brief overview of each ground's history allied to one or two historical photographs. It is hoped, however, that this brief selection will provide readers with an awareness of the scale of a number of grounds outside the Football League and this history of some of the clubs associated with them.

This book is published shortly after the completion of the first wholly new major league ground in the Metropolis – Arsenal's new Emirates Stadium – since World War 2 and as the new Wembley gradually moves towards completion. It is fortunate that the history of both of these grounds, and of their predecessors, are well recorded in the Aerofilms' archive as, with the demolition of one and conversion of the other, there is an undoubted feel that part of London's heritage has been lost. Whilst personal memories of visits to these classic grounds may fade over a period of time, the beauty of photography is that it freezes, for perpetuity, a moment in time.

This book is also being published contemporaneously with another event. For commercial reasons, the owners of the Aerofilms company have decided to cease the library's operations during the summer of 2006. What the future holds for the archive at the time of going to press is uncertain. Ian Allan Publishing has worked closely with the library over many years in the compilation of books drawing upon the archive's phenomenal collections for more than two decades and have produced a large number of books drawn from it. At this juncture, it is only

Brentford
1996
(656178; see pp22-27)

right that we thank the company and its staff for their assistance over the years. In particular, we'd like to thank the current librarian, Chris Mawson, for all his help with the most recent titles; there must have been times when last-minute requests for obscure dates from the registers must have proved distracting but the answers were always forthcoming. To Aerofilms, and especially to Chris, many thanks for all your help.

ARSENAL

Founded in 1886 as Royal Arsenal and becoming Woolwich Arsenal before joining the Football League in 1893, by March 1910 the club was in dire straits and, in that month, went into voluntary liquidation. The club was rescued by Henry Norris, who controlled Fulham and saw in a merger between the two clubs the opportunity of bringing First Division football to Craven Cottage. In the event, the merger did not proceed but relocation did. After a somewhat hurried period of construction, the new Arsenal Stadium, as Highbury should be referred to, opened on 6 September 1913. It boasted – if that is the right word – a Main (East) Stand designed by Archibald Leitch and open terracing on the three other sides; this had been constructing using spoil from the construction of the Piccadilly Line and by levelling the pitch.

This is the condition shown in this view of Highbury taken in 1923.
1923 (9247)

During the years of Herbert Chapman's management the ground was transformed. In 1931, under the aegis of the architect Claude Waterlow Ferrier, both end terraces were enlarged and, in 1932, the superb West Stand was completed; the new stand was opened officially on 10 December 1932. This view, taken shortly before the opening of the West Stand, shows work nearing completion as well as the expanded terraces at the North and South ends.

28 September 1932
(40600 [C19089])

The North Bank was covered in 1935. After this, the old Main Stand was demolished (in April 1936) and the new stand, similar in style to the West Stand, was designed by William Binnie and opened on 24 October 1936. This view, again taken shortly before work on the new stand was completed, illustrates the ground as it existed until World War 2.

27 August 1936
(R2245)

▲ **D**uring the war, the cover over the North End was removed as this view, taken shortly after the war shows.

1949
(A21415 [C19947])

▶ **T**he roof over the North End was rebuilt in 1954.

20 June 1957
(A67822)

Fifteen years later the ground is still largely unchanged with the open terrace at the South End, the covered terrace at the North and the two stands on the West and East sides.

18 August 1972
(A243930)

Radical change to Highbury came with the requirement to convert the ground to all-seater following the various disasters that affected football in the 1980s. Seating was installed in both the West and East stands and, in 1989, the terrace at the South End was replaced by the Clock End Stand with its executive boxes, although the roof provided did not cover the seats in front of the boxes. This view, taken in 1992, shows the new Clock End Stand along with the site of the now-demolished North Bank.

14 September 1992
(613864)

The new North Stand, which represented the final development of Highbury, was opened on 14 August 1993. The ground now had an all-seater capacity of some 38,900 – increasingly limited as other Premier League grounds expanded. During the 1999/2000 season it was announced that the club intended to relocate. This view records Highbury as it appeared during its final decade following the construction of the new North Stand.

26 May 2001
(688311)

The close proximity of Highbury to the new ground is evident in this view taken of construction of the new stadium at Ashburton Grove in mid-2005.

27 May 2005
(699022)

Although the process took slightly longer than the club originally anticipated, the new Emirates Stadium, with its 60,000 all-seater capacity, opened at the start of the 2006/07 season with Highbury seeing its final game in the 4-1 victory over Wigan at the end of the 2005/06 season. Although Highbury will be redeveloped as flats, much of the structure, being listed, will be incorporated into the new work.

25 May 2006
(700185)

The history of Underhill as a football ground dates back to 1906 and the establishment of Barnet Alston. The club moved to Underhill the following year and the first game was played at the new ground on 14 September 1907. In 1912 Barnet Alston merged with Barnet FC – the second club to bear that name – to form Barnet & Alston FC; the name was changed to Barnet in 1919. This first view shows the ground as it existed in the late 1960s when Barnet had become one of the most successful non-league teams in Britain. Floodlights were installed in 1962, whilst between 1964 and 1967 the new Main Stand, replacing that constructed in 1926, was constructed. Also built during these years were the covers on the East and South sides.

21 May 1969
(A197812)

Some 20 years later Underhill was still in this condition when Barnet were admitted to the Football League in 1991 although to achieve the League's minimum standard for seating accommodation, an additional 273 seats were bolted on to the existing terraces.

14 September 1992

(613883)

In 1993 the roof over the South Terrace was removed and the terrace was dismantled; it was replaced by temporary uncovered seating in 1995, a facility that is still subject to annual permit. The club returned to the League for the start of the 2005/06 season, having been relegated in 2000/01, and this view shows the ground as it existed at the time of the club's return to the League. There remain problems with the ground's capacity and access and the club is actively seeking to relocate although it has not, as yet, proved possible to find a suitable site within the borough. If this search ultimately proves hopeless, then the club may well seek to ground share elsewhere or build a new ground away from its traditional home.

21 June 2005
(699359)

BRENTFORD

Founded in 1889, it was not until 1904 that Brentford moved to Griffin Park, playing its first game there on 1 September of that year. In 1920 the club joined the Third Division of the Football League and it is from this period, and the club's remarkable rise to the First Division by the early 1930s, that the ground as illustrated in this early 1950s photograph shows. In 1927 a new Main Stand was constructed. This was followed in 1931 by the installation of a cover over the New Road Terrace (opposite the Main Stand). The Brook Road End was roofed in two stages in 1933 and 1935 whilst in the latter year seating was installed in the wings adjacent to the Main Stand.

Early 1950s
(F41C)

The only major change between the mid-1930s and the date of this photograph was the installation of floodlights in 1954.

1 July 1957
(A68141)

In February 1983, part of the Main Stand was destroyed by fire; the rebuilt section – distinguishable because of the changed roofline – was reopened at the start of the 1984/85 season. Following the Bradford City fire, the ground's capacity was reduced to 9,500 and the ground was under further threat after the Taylor Report, when the capacity of the Ealing Terrace was reduced to only 793 from 4,000. Apart from the Main Stand, other significant changes included the sale of land behind the Brook Road Terrace in 1985 and this sale generated the funds to enable the building of the small two-tier structure; this opened in late 1986. Also in 1986, the rear section of the New Road Terrace was dismantled and the roof cut back; this area has subsequently had seating fitted. In 1991/92 the seating in the Main Stand was increased. The Ealing Terrace has had work undertaken on it in order to increase capacity, but plans for the construction of a new stand were rejected by Hounslow Council following objections from local residents.

7 September 1992

(613797)

The club is faced by the fact that it occupies a confined space with little scope for development and has had tentative plans for relocation since the late 1980s with the current preferred location being sited close to Kew Bridge where a 25,000-seat ground is proposed, although there is as yet no timescale for any work. In the meantime, there are proposals for the further development at Griffin Road with planned work including modification of the New Road Stand and the provision of a roof over the Ealing Road Terrace. Although the original application was rejected by the planning authorities in December 2004, following local consultation plans were approved in mid-April 2005. The work will ultimately result in a capacity of 15,000 at Griffin Park. One thing that does change regularly at Griffin Park, however, is the roof advertising, with companies taking advantage of the club's position on the direct flightpath into Heathrow. At the time of going to press the current advertiser was Qatar Airways.

25 May 2006
(700196)

CHARLTON ATHLETIC

Although The Valley could lay claim to being probably, in capacity terms, the largest ground in the Football League, the actual facilities offered were poor for many years. Charlton Athletic itself was formed in 1905, but did not play its first game at The Valley until 13 September 1919. Two years later the team entered the Football League. The ground as illustrated in this photograph from the early 1930s shows the Main Stand with its four-span roof on the west side; this was constructed contemporaneously with the club's entry into the Football League.

5 April 1933
(40932)

By the early 1960s, as shown in this view, the ground was still relatively basic. Apart from the Main Stand the only other covered accommodation was provided on the North Terrace, which was covered in 1934 (and damaged during the war). The huge East Terrace was completed during the 1930s, whilst in 1950 seats were installed in the Main Stand Paddock. Floodlighting was installed at the ground in 1961 shortly before this photograph was taken.

31 August 1961
(A96421)

A decade later, the ground remained primitive and would remain so for much of the 1970's.

20 July 1970
(A208189)

On 21 September 1985 the club left The Valley, to begin a seven-year period of exile, initially at Crystal Palace and later at Upton Park. The campaign to see the team return to The Valley was long drawn out, highly political and eventually successful. The end result was that the team returned to The Valley in late 1992, playing its first game back there on 5 December 1992. In returning to The Valley the club was faced by many of the problems over the ground which had existed prior to its departure and which had remained unsolved during the club's absence. Of the ground that existed prior to the club's exile, only one element – the South Stand – is largely unchanged. The South (Jimmy Seed) Stand was opened in August 1981 replacing the original open terrace. The original Main (West) Stand roof had been replaced in 1979 and again a decade later; this structure, described as temporary, was to last almost a decade. The only part of the ground that could not be used when the ground reopened was the East Terrace, which was not to last long after this photograph was taken.

14 September 1992
(614075)

The new East Stand, which replaced the old East
Terrace (the one part of the ground that could not be
reopened in 1992 and which was demolished in 1993),
was opened on 2 April 1994.

26 March 1994
(627020)

Work started at the Valley in early 1998 on the construction of a new West Stand; this was completed later that year and took the ground's capacity to fractionally over 20,000. In early 2001, following the granting of planning permission, work commenced on the construction of a new 6,500-seat North Stand.

26 May 2001
(688363)

The construction of the North Stand, costing £9 million, was completed for the 2001/02 season and took the ground's capacity to 26,500. Further planned work will see the ground's capacity increase ultimately to 40,000. This work will include the construction of a further tier on the East Stand and the complete rebuilding of the South Stand in two phases.

27 May 2005
(699296)

CHELSEA

Stamford Bridge's sporting life started in 1877 as an athletics circuit – an activity that was to continue until 1932 – and it was not until 1905 that Chelsea was established to play football at the ground. Stamford Bridge saw its first football match on 4 September 1905; Chelsea was admitted at the start of the 1905/06 season to the Second Division of the Football League. The ground as illustrated in 1935 shows how relatively primitive the facilities were at the time, with the only covered accommodation being provided by the 1905 East Stand (designed by Archibald Leitch) and by the curious cover at the rear of the Fulham Road End. The latter, known as the Shed, was built in 1935 and was thus new at the time of the photograph. The fact that the ground's origins lay in an athletics circuit is evident; the track was also used for greyhound racing (until 1968) and for speedway (between 1928 and 1932).

1935

The facilities at Stamford Bridge continued to be relatively poor as shown in this view taken in 1980. The only significant change to the ground shown 45 years earlier is the replacement of the East Stand. This structure replaced the original Leitch structure (demolished in mid-1972) and opened in August 1974. However, the costs involved in the construction of the new ground were one factor in the emerging financial crisis that at one stage threatened not only the ground but the club itself.

1980
(SV10303)

The first phase in what proved to be the massive redevelopment of Stamford Bridge began in a small way in the early 1990s with the refurbishment of the East Stand and the provision of new seating. It is this that is recorded in this 1994 view.

7 September 1994
(614380)

The ground has been largely redeveloped since 1993 under the concept of the 'Chelsea Village' promoted by former chairman Ken Bates, which included plans for a hotel, flats, and underground car park as well as a 40,000-seat stadium. In order to accommodate all these elements, the pitch has been reduced in size and the oval circuit has disappeared. Work started on the new North Stand in December 1993; the main section opened in November 1994. In the summer of 1994 the Shed was removed and the Fulham Road (South Bank) End modified to allow for temporary seating. This is the stage recorded in this 1995 view.

10 March 1995
(639054)

The corner section at the northwest corner adjacent to the new North Stand opened in 1996. Work started on the underground car park behind the South Bank in 1995 and the new South Stand and associated hotel were constructed in 1996-7. Finally, in 1997, work started on the new West Stand. This work was long drawn out as – inevitably given the story of Chelsea – there was a dispute over the final form that the stand would take. Initially permission was granted for the construction of the lower tier only, which was left open to the elements, and which gave Stamford Bridge a capacity of 35,629. The new South Stand and open lower tier of the West Stand can be seen to good effect in this view taken in 1998 looking towards the northwest.

8 May 1998
(674580)

However, planning disputes mean that the West Stand was destined to remain uncompleted for several seasons and it was only in 2000 that work recommenced on the completion of the stand. The impressive two-tier stand was completed during the course of the 2000/01 season and completed current redevelopment work on the actual stadium at Stamford Bridge and took the ground's capacity to 42,449. Ken Bates sold the club to Russian entrepreneur Roman Abramovich in 2003 and, now backed by Abramovich, the club has raised its aspirations. There is talk of further development at Stamford Bridge or possibly of relocation, although nothing is at present confirmed.

25 May 2006
(700207)

CRYSTAL PALACE

Although based at Selhurst Park for more than 70 years, the origins of the club – as its name implies – go back to the famous Crystal Palace designed by Sir Joseph Paxton for the Great Exhibition of 1851. The present club, however, was only established in 1904 and, after an itinerant life, played its first game at the new Selhurst Park on 30 August 1924, having joined the Football League in 1920. At the time that the ground was opened, the facilities provided were an Archibald Leitch-designed Main Stand on the west and three sides of banking. As can be seen in this photograph, 25 years after the club moved to Selhurst Park the Main Stand remained the only covered accommodation although proper terracing had been installed along the lower sections of the other three sides of the ground. For the club's early years, these facilities, whilst rudimentary, probably sufficed; however, in the 1960s the club started an inexorable climb up the Football League and, by the end of the decade, had reached the old First Division.

1949
(HAS/UK/49/217))

From the late 1960s onwards there have been significant developments at Selhurst Park. In addition to the physical changes at the ground, since 1985 Selhurst Park has also been shared by two other teams: Charlton Athletic from 1985 until 1991 and Wimbledon from 1992 until 2002. The original 1924 stand remains, although it is now all seater (with seating installed in its paddock in 1979 and with a hospitality suite built behind it in 1992/93). Opposite this is the Arthur Wait Stand (on the Park Road Side); this was initially built in 1969 and in 1990 was converted to an all-seater arrangement. The Whitehorse Lane (North) End was redeveloped in 1981; a reduced terrace was constructed with housing and a supermarket located behind. The Whitehorse Lane End was further modified in 1991 and 1992 by the addition of executive boxes and by being converted to an all-seater arrangement.

26 March 1994
(626985)

The final development occurred in 1994/95 with the construction of the new Holmesdale Road Stand. This took the ground's capacity to 26,400 all seated.

31 January 1996
(654371)

There are long term plans for the redevelopment of the Main Stand (for which planning permission has been obtained), but there is no confirmed timetable at this stage and it is strongly opposed by local residents. If the club does not expand at Selhurst Park, then it may well seek to relocate. The situation at Selhurst Park is complicated by the fact that ownership of the ground is controlled by former club chairman, Ron Noades, whilst Palace itself is now controlled by Michael Jordan.

25 May 2006
(700216)

FULHAM

Fulham FC was established as St Andrews in 1879; after moving to Craven Cottage in 1894, the club played its first game at the ground on 10 October 1896. The club joined the Football League in 1907. The rudimentary facilities offered at Craven Cottage in its earliest years are shown to good effect in this 1928 view. As illustrated, Craven Cottage was still very much the product of Archibald Leitch's involvement in the first decade of the 20th century. In 1905, before the club joined the League, Leitch designed the famous corner pavilion, as well as the Stevenage Road Stand and the three open sides: the Riverside Terrace alongside the Thames, the Hammersmith and Putney ends.

30 May 1928
(21441)

Thirty years later the scene at Craven Cottage is unchanged; the three terraces remain open to the elements whilst both the cottage and Stevenage Road Stand would be instantly recognised by Leitch if he had been able to return to the ground.

12 May 1958
(A70736)

Progress came slowly to Craven Cottage. The
Riverside Terrace was roofed in April 1972 – as the
Eric Miller Stand (named after one erstwhile chairman)
The corner pavilion and Stevenage Road Stand were
both listed in March 1987. The Hammersmith End was
extended in 1961 and covered at the rear four years
later. Floodlighting was installed in 1962.

7 September 1992
(614118)

Seats were installed on the Riverside Terrace in 1997 and work was also undertaken to upgrade the Stevenage Road Stand. In 1998 revolution came to Craven Cottage when Harrods boss Mohamed Al-Fayed took over. With his backing the club moved from the Second to the First Division at the end of the 1998/99 season and, two years later, up to the Premiership, bringing back terraces for one season to English football's top flight. However, the club's rapid rise brought with it the need to redevelop its ground and the club had ambitious plans for the reconstruction of the ground with planning permission being granted towards the end of the 2000/01 season for the construction of a 30,000 all-seater stadium costing £55 million on the existing site. All of the existing ground – including the famous cottage – was to have been swept away with the exception of the facade along Stevenage Road. It was anticipated that work would commence at the end of the 2001/02 season with Fulham ground sharing during the 2002/03 season, prior to occupying its new facility in August 2003.

27 June 2000
(685842)

In the event, however, the planned redevelopment at Craven Cottage or the club's possible relocation failed to progress as planned and, after two years, the club returned to Craven Cottage at the start of the 2004/05 season. In order to facilitate the club's return the Hammersmith End was reroofed and the Putney End covered for the first time. Seating was installed under the new covers at both ends, giving Craven Cottage an all-seated capacity of 22,480. This is small, however, by Premier League standards.

25 May 2006
(700232)

A member of the Football League since 1905, Clapton – later Leyton – Orient first played at Millfields Road in 1896. The ground had been used for whippet racing prior to the football club's arrival. The early facilities were rudimentary, comprising little more than four embankments and a covered press box. The next phase of development was the construction of a 2,000-seat South Stand in 1906; this structure was to be sold to Wimbledon in 1923 and re-erected at Plough Lane at which stage a new stand was constructed. The major development of the ground occurred after 1927 when greyhound racing, courtesy of the Clapton Stadium Syndicate, was introduced. The ground as illustrated in this photograph taken looking towards the 1923-built South Stand shows well the changes brought about by the arrival of the greyhounds: the rebuilt oval track; concrete terracing around the ground; and, increased covered accommodation. Orient's occupation, however, was drawing to a close and, on 3 May 1930, the club played its last match at the ground, relocating to the Lea Bridge Stadium for the 1930/31 season. Greyhound racing continued at Millfields Road for more than four decades. After closure, the site was cleared and used for housing.

4 August 1954
(A55972)

LEYTON ORIENT

Pictured in October 1930, the old Wembley Stadium had a brief career as a venue for League football as Clapton Orient played two games on the hallowed turf in November 1930 as the pitch at its own Lea Bridge Stadium was deemed to be too narrow. The full story of Wembley Stadium is told on pp106-114.

9 October 1930
(34580)

In 1930 Clapton (now Leyton) Orient moved to the Lea Bridge Stadium from its earlier Millfields Road ground. By this date, the Lea Bridge Stadium, viewed here looking towards the south, was already in use as a speedway track and boasted a covered Main (South) Stand. However, the Football League was not satisfied with the size of the pitch and, for a couple of matches, Orient was forced to play two home games at Wembley whilst work was undertaken at the Lea Bridge Stadium. Later improvements saw the construction of a small covered stand on the East Side and concrete terracing around most, but not all, of the perimeter. Orient continued to play matches at the Lea Bridge Stadium until the end of the 1936/37 season when the club relocated to its current ground a Brisbane Road. Speedway continued at the Lea Bridge stadium until after World War 2; when this ceased, the ground was demolished and redeveloped.

June 1933
(42089)

For the first 50 years of its life, Leyton Orient (as it became after World War 2 and again after 1987) occupied a number of grounds before settling at Brisbane Road in 1937. The club replaced the Leyton Amateurs at Brisbane Road, playing its first game there on 28 August 1937. The Amateurs had played at Brisbane Road since 1905. Orient inherited a ground with a stand on one side – the west – and with terraces on the remaining three sides. The 'This shot, taken shortly before Orient's one and only season in the First Division, shows both the old West Stand and the new East (Main) Stand, which had been built in 1956 and which was damaged by fire on completion. Floodlights had been inaugurated earlier in 1960.

28 June 1960
(A81492)

Thirty years later, the ground was largely unchanged
except that the East Stand was extended in 1962
however, it would not be long before change occurred.

14 September 1992

(613890)

The East Stand had been extended in 1962 and, whilst not clearly visible here, seats were installed in the West Stand in 1977. The major difference by 2000 was the disappearance of the South Terrace and its replacement by a new small South Stand. The old terrace was demolished in 1996 and the site stood empty for a couple of seasons. The original plans envisaged the construction of a 3,000-seat stand on the site, but in the event these proposals had to be scaled down and a 1,300-seat structure – illustrated here – was completed for the 1999/2000 season.

7 May 2000
(695629)

The club – which was acquired by Barry Hearn in March 1995 – had plans for the further redevelopment of the ground and received a £1 million grant from the Football Trust for the construction of a new West Stand in December 2000. The next phase in the ground's redevelopment was the rebuilding of the West Stand and North Terrace. The north and west sides of the ground were cleared during 2004.

2004
(697666)

The new West Stand, constructed during the 2004/05 season, added 2,500 to the ground's capacity and also housed club offices and other facilities. The provision of rental office space in the West Stand was designed to raise income that was designed to help fund the construction of a new North Stand.

27 May 2005
(699331)

Work at Brisbane Road during the 2005/06 season included the construction of residential blocks at each corner of the ground. The next phase of the ground's development will be the construction of the new North Stand.

25 May 2006
(700237)

MILLWALL

Founded on the Isle of Dogs (north of the River Thames) in 1885, it was not until 22 October 1910 that Millwall migrated south of the river and played its first game at The Den. At that date the ground consisted of three open terraces and a Main Stand designed by Archibald Leitch. Ten years after moving to The Den, Millwall joined the Football League. During the late 1930s, covered accommodation was provided at the rear of the three open sides. Although this view does not encompass the whole of the Den, it does show to good effect the size of open terracing on the east side of the ground and the close proximity of the ground to New Cross Stadium.

29 June 1935
(R834)

However, during one fateful week in 1943, the ground suffered severe damage. Firstly, a bomb attack saw the cover over the North Terrace destroyed whilst, a week later, a fire caused by a cigarette caused severe damage to the Leitch-designed Main Stand. Millwall was forced temporarily to vacate the ground – playing its games for a period at Charlton's Valley ground. The wartime damage took a number of years to repair completely, although Millwall's exile was relatively short-lived. Floodlighting was first installed in 1953 and in 1962 the Main Stand was fully seated and reroofed. This is the condition shown in this view from 1964.

18 April 1964
(A125504)

Although there have been a number of cases where local authorities have thwarted the efforts of clubs either to modernise existing grounds or to relocate to new stadia, in the case of Millwall, Lewisham Council proved highly co-operative. The last major change came at the original ground in 1985 when an extension was built to the North Terrace roof to provide a new family section. The major impetus for redevelopment at Millwall came with the club's success in reaching the old First Division – ironically the last London league team to achieve that status – when it was faced with making the ground all-seater. While it would have been practical (if expensive) to have rebuilt the original ground, the decision was taken to build a brand new stadium. The original ground was sold to a housing company, Fairview Homes, and on 8 May 1993 Millwall played its last game at its home for more than 80 years. This view shows how close the old and new grounds were to each other; note also that the New Cross Stadium has been demolished. This was to disappear in 1975.

17 June 1993

(620290)

The new ground, designed by the Miller Partnership, is provided with stands on all four sides; the total, all-seater, capacity is 20,150. The first game played at the new ground was a friendly against Sporting Lisbon on 4 August 1993.

20 March 1997

(664668)

In the years since Millwall moved to the new ground, there has been relatively little development except for the provision of a protected footpath for use by away fans.

15 June 2003
(697383)

QUEENS PARK RANGERS

Although based at Loftus Road for more than 80 years, Queens Park Rangers dates back to a merger in 1886 between two teams (St Judes and Christchurch Rangers) and is a club that has led a somewhat nomadic existence. Even after moving to Loftus Road – where it played its first game on 8 September 1917 (although Shepherd's Bush had been playing there since 1904) – QPR has had two spells of playing at the White City Stadium – in 1931/32 and 1962/63 – and in the mid-1960s there were plans to make the move permanent. This view shows Loftus Road as it existed in the late 1920s, shortly after QPR joined the Third Division in 1920. The ground was provided with three open terraces, whilst the fourth side – along Ellerslie Road – was provided with a cover in 1917 that had been transferred from QPR's previous ground at Park Royal. The foreground is dominated by the exhibition halls associated with the White City complex; these were to disappear in the 1930s when the blocks of flats evident in the more recent photographs were constructed.

1928
(22720)

Built for the Olympic Games of 1908, the White City Stadium played host to League football on two occasions when QPR were tenants of the Greyhound Racing Association (who had acquired the stadium in 1930). Although QPR had first played football at the stadium in 1912 when the club was in the Southern League, QPR played its first League match at the ground on 5 September 1931. The photograph is contemporary with this first spell as a League club at White City. It shows clearly the covered terraces constructed following the GRA's acquisition of the stadium; at this stage the ground's capacity was 80,000 but the photograph also makes clear that, whilst the White City Stadium had better facilities and a greater capacity than Loftus Road, the distance from the pitch and the low attendances achieved meant that the atmosphere was poor. As a result, the club reverted to Loftus Road at the end of the 1931/32 season. Thirty years later, in 1962/63, QPR again played its home matches at White City; by this date the stadium had been fully covered and there were some 11,000 seats within the total capacity of 60,000. Again, however, the experiment proved unsuccessful and the club played its last match at White City on 22 May 1963. Although football was still to be played at the stadium – including the World Cup of 1966 – this was to be the end of White City in terms of League football. White City, however, continued to provide a home for greyhound racing, speedway and athletics before its final closure in 1984. The site was subsequently demolished and used for the expansion of BBC facilities.

1931

(36467)

The more recent photographs show the results of the club's rebuilding programme from 1968 onwards. The first phase of this work saw the opening of the South Africa Road (North) Stand in 1968. This was followed in 1972 by the Ellerslie Road (South) Stand. The two-tier Loftus Road (East) End Stand was completed in 1980, Finally, in 1981, the School End was completed.

1992
(614103)

The School End was further upgraded in 1993 and the lower tier of the Loftus Road (East) Stand was fitted with seats in 1994. This is the condition of the ground shown in this 2004 view. Today, Loftus Road has an all-seater capacity of 19,148 and, apart from QPR, is also used for Rugby Union matches and, during two seasons from 2002 to 2004, it was also home to Premiership side Fulham. As can be seen the ground is in a confined location and this has led the club to contemplate the possibility – but no more than this at the current time – of relocation given that the current capacity is relatively small and there is no real potential for further development at Loftus Road.

19 November 2004
(698101)

Paradoxically not the home of West Ham United but of Thames FC, the West Ham Stadium was completed in 1928 and, with a notional capacity of some 120,000, was one of the largest grounds constructed in the United Kingdom. In footballing terms, however, it never justified this capacity as, during its short League career, Thames never achieved a gate of more than 8,275. The ground as built was designed to accommodate both speedway and greyhound racing as well as football and was provided with covered seating accommodation on both sides and covered terracing at the north. Thames was admitted to Division Three (S) in 1930 but folded at the end of the 1931/32 season and did not seek re-election. As a greyhound and speedway stadium, the ground remained until the 1970s. It was subsequently demolished and the site utilised for housing.

The view taken here shows the ground in 1928 shortly after its completion.

1928
(24264)

TOTTENHAM HOTSPUR

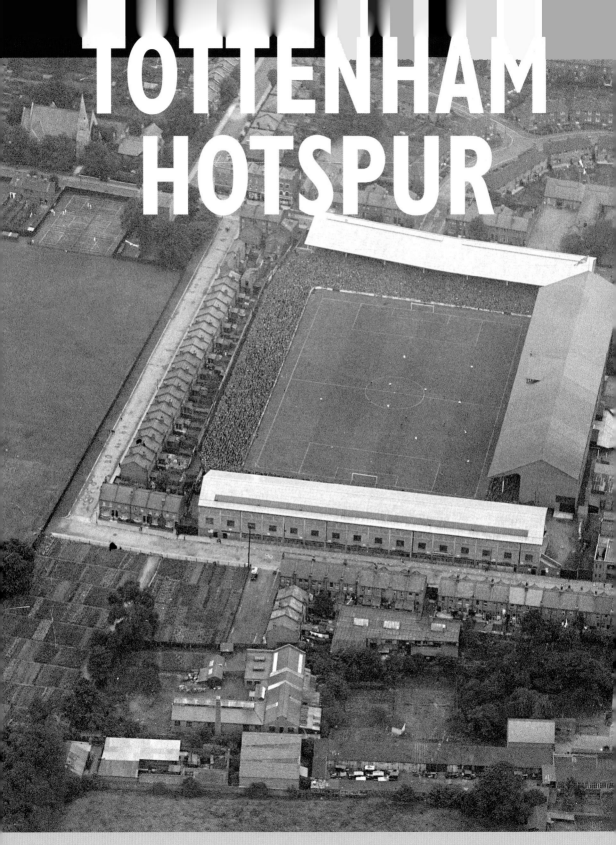

Although founded as Hotspur FC in 1882, the name was changed to Tottenham Hotspur three years later. The club moved to the future White Hart Lane in 1899, playing its first game there on 4 September 1899. Almost a decade later, in 1908, the club was admitted to the Football League. The ground as originally developed was very much the product of the famous ground designer Archibald Leitch. Leitch's involvement with the ground started in 1909 with the completion of the West Stand – the structure with the Tottenham Hotspur Football Club lettering. In 1921 the Paxton Road (North) End was covered; this was followed two years later by the Park Lane (South) End. Again both these covers were designed by Leitch. This is the condition portrayed in this view taken in the early 1920s looking towards the south.

1923
(9243)

Leitch's final involvement with the ground came in 1934 with the completion of the East Stand and this is reflected in the condition of the ground shown in this view taken shortly after World War 2 looking towards the north west.

18 August 1951
(R15398)

Floodlighting was first installed in 1953 but by the start of the following decade the ground was still identifiably that originally designed by Archibald Leitch.

31 August 1961
(A96459)

During the 1960s, seating was installed in the rear parts of both ends although there is little evidence of change over the previous decade in this view from the early 1970s other than the extension of the West Stand towards the north (completed in 1972 and clearly shown by the different roof colour).

13 July 1972
(A233895)

The major transformation of White Hart Lane started in 1980 with the demolition of the West Stand; the new structure was opened in February 1982. In 1987 plans were unveiled to refurbish the East Stand; work started on this in March 1989 and the new facility was opened the following October. Like all teams in the top two divisions, Spurs were faced by the need to become all-seater. As a result seats were installed during 1992 in the lower tier of the East Side and in the lower section of the Park Lane End. The final section to be converted was the remainder of the East Side, which was undertaken in 1994 just before the deadline. In the meantime, a new roof was constructed at the Paxton Road End; this was completed in 1993 and this is the condition reflected in this view taken in 1994.

26 March 1994
(626837)

The next phase in the development of the ground, in 1995, was the construction of the South Stand.

28 February 1998
(673567)

Today, White Hart Lane's capacity is 36,257 (all-seated). The club was taken over during the 2000/01 season and the new owners announced in March 2001 that they were investigating the possibility of relocation. Unlike north London rivals Arsenal, however, Tottenham's plans have yet to be fully developed. In October 2001 planning permission was granted for the construction of a third tier on the East Stand, taking capacity to 44,000, as a temporary measure whilst relocation was further investigated. This work, however, had no timescale and has not, as yet, been undertaken. It would appear that the club remains committed to relocation, with the new Wembley one possibility, although there are no definite plans.

25 May 2006
(700258)

Although the club has its origins in the 1880s, it was not until 1920 that Watford joined the Third Division of the Football League and not until 30 August 1922 did it play its first game at Vicarage Road. The first view of the ground, albeit dating from the late 1940s, shows Vicarage Road very much as it developed in 1920. At the centre of the East Side was a 45yd-long stand (this was extended to the south in 1969). Opposite was the Shrodells (West) Stand; this had been transferred from the earlier Cassio Road ground as had the short cover at the Rookery (South) End. The Vicarage Road End was built up with hard-core (later concreted) for terracing and concrete terracing was also installed between the Shrodells Stand and the Rookery End (in the 1930s). The ground's shape also owes much to the fact that, from 1928 until 1969 and from 1975 until it finally ceased in 1978, Vicarage Road was used for greyhound racing.

10 September 1949
(A26501)

More than a decade later, Vicarage Road was still largely unchanged except for the construction of a cover over the terrace at the Rookery (South) End in 1959 and the provision of new floodlights in 1960.

9 September 1964
(A138602)

There have been radical changes to Vicarage Road over the past quarter of a century. Although the East Stand and its 1969 extension survive, these have been fitted with seats throughout. The first phase of the ground's modernisation came with the opening of the Sir Stanley Rous (West) Stand on 18 October 1986. This was followed in October 1993 by the opening of the North Stand (replacing the Vicarage Road Terrace). This is the condition recorded in this 1994 view.

1994
(626929)

The next phase in the development of Vicarage Road came in March 1995 with the construction the new South Stand (replacing the Rookery End). Today, Watford has a capacity of 22,100 all seated. Whilst the club had planned previously to rebuild the East Stand, the club's financial position, exacerbated by the demise of ITV Digital, meant that the project was put on ice.

25 May 2006
(699842)

WEST HAM UNITED

Football Grounds in London from the Air

West Ham United was formed as Thames Ironworks in September 1895 and joined the Southern League in 1898. The club became West Ham United in 1900 and moved to the Boleyn Ground – as Upton Park should be properly called – in May 1904, playing its first game there on 1 September the same year. The Hammers joined the Football League in 1919. The ground in 1957 comprised the double-deck West Stand, which was originally built in 1925 and which is being extended here. The South Bank roof was transferred from the old (1913) West Stand in 1925; this suffered war damage in 1944 but was repaired. The narrow East Side was covered during the mid-1920s; as a result of the materials used in the building's construction, it became known as the 'Chicken Run'.

19 August 1957

(A68822)

Taken in the mid-1960s, this view shows work in progress on the extension, by one bay, of the West Stand. Earlier in the decade, in 1961, the North Bank had been covered.

10 June 1965
(A150665)

In May 1968 the 'Chicken Run' was demolished to be replaced by a new East Stand which opened in January 1969; this is the new structure shown in this view taken from early in the following decade.

13 July 1972
(A233752)

In the mid-1970s seats were fitted in the West Stand paddock and the capacity in the North Bank was reduced as the ground became governed by the Safety at Sports Grounds Act. The major development, however, came after the acquisition of the old school site in 1991 and the launch of the highly controversial bond scheme. The £5.5 million Bobby Moore (North) Stand – named after the late West Ham and England captain – was opened in February 1994. The East Stand was fully fitted with seats in 1994. The South Bank was demolished in May 1993 with the new Centenary Stand being opened in February 1995 shortly before the date of this photograph.

15 May 1995

(642122)

The work in the mid-1990s resulted in the ground having a capacity of just over 26,000, making it relatively small in Premiership terms and the club developed plans for the further expansion of the stadium. Work started on the new West Stand in January 2001. This view, taken early in 2001, shows works in progress on the construction of the new stand.

26 May 2001
(688675)

The new West Stand – called the Dr Martens Stand – was completed by the start of the 2001/02 season and saw the ground's capacity increased from 26,100 to 35,000. Following the construction of the Dr Martens Stand, the club turned its attention to the East Stand and undertake work on the Bobby Moore and Centenary stands, with the intention of raising the capacity to more than 40,000. The total cost of these proposed new stands is £35 million and plans were submited following the team's promotion to the Premiership in May 2005.

27 May 2005
(699346)

The home of Wimbledon FC, Plough Lane became a Football League ground in 1977 when the team was elected to membership of League Division Four when it replaced Workington Town, thus beginning one of the strangest stories in Football League history. Plough Lane was first used for football in 1912 and by the early 1930s comprised stands on the north and south side (the latter being acquired second-hand from Clapton Orient's ground at Millfields Road in 1923), with banking at the west end and terracing at the east. The photograph, taken looking towards the north, shows the ground as it existed following a period of considerable investment, reflected in the fact that many of the facilities look new. As a result of the generosity of Sydney Black, the ground had undergone significant development during the late 1950s, during which time (in 1959) the club acquired the freehold of the site. This work included the construction of the Main (North) Stand in 1958, the building of the Sportsman Pub at the northwest corner, the construction of a cantilevered roof over the West Terrace in 1959 and the installation of floodlights in 1960.

5 May 1961
(A87219)

Following the club's relocation in 1991 (it moved to share Selhurst Park with Crystal Palace at the start of the 1991/92 season prior to moving to Milton Keynes when plans for a possible return to the Borough of Merton fell through), Plough Lane continued in use for football for some years for reserve matches; however, this has now ceased and the ground was demolished in 2002 for redevelopment. This view, taken in 1965 shortly after the club turned professional, looking towards the southwest, also shows, in the foreground, Wimbledon Stadium, which was used for greyhound racing.

20 June 1965
(A146992)

Destined to become one of the most famous football grounds in the world, Wembley Stadium was designed by Simpson in connection with the British Empire Exhibition held in 1925. This view, taken in the autumn of 1922, shows construction of the ground with, closest to the camera, work progressing on the foundations of what would later become the most iconic feature of this famous ground – the twin towers. This view is instructional in that it shows clearly the method of construction. The lower levels of the terraces were based on a base constructed of spoil; the upper levels used steel framing covering with concrete panels. The rapidity of construction was such that the new ground was available to host the FA Cup Final of 1923 – the famous 'White horse' match between West Ham United and Bolton Wanderers.

5 September 1922
(C14257)

The completed Wembley Stadium pictured in 1924 with many of the pavilions and other buildings also constructed for the Empire exhibition in the background. The vast open terraces are a reminder of the era when the ground's capacity was 100,000, although the record attendance was 126,047 for the first FA Cup Final to be staged at the ground in 1923.

1924
(10845)

Although traditionally the home of major domestic and international football and Rugby League matches, arguably Wembley's finest moment – other than England's triumph in the 1966 World Cup Final – came on 29 July 1948 when the famous ground played host to the opening ceremony of the 1948 Olympic Games. This view, taken on the day, records the vast crowds both inside and outside the stadium to witness this momentous event.

29 July 1948
(A17616/48)

The ground was fully covered in 1963; at that time
some 44,000 of the ground's capacity was seated.

12 April 1963
(A109561)

In the mid-1970s, in order to improve access to the ground and crowd safety, a walkway was constructed leading towards the ground along Olympic Way from Wembley Park station. This 1976 view sees the walkway under construction. In the right foreground can be seen the Empire Pool and Arena.

1976
(A313680)

Wembley became an all-seater stadium in 1990 and, in order to provide an additional 4,000 seats, the Olympic Gallery was constructed. From the mid-1980s onwards some £40 million was spent at Wembley, resulting in an all-seater capacity of 80,000.

10 March 1995

(639003)

► **D**espite its pedigree, however, Wembley was increasingly showing its age; modern regulations had seen the ground's capacity cut and plans were formulated for the wholesale redevelopment of the ground. In order to gain National Lottery funding for the construction of a new national stadium, ownership of Wembley was transferred to the English National Stadium Trust during 1998. Once the transfer was completed, plans for the ground's redevelopment were, in theory, finalised but problems over the cost of the scheme resulted in delays even after the final game played at the ground – a World Cup qualifier against Germany on 2 October 2000 (a game that

resulted in an England defeat and the resignation of then manager Kevin Keegan). The old ground remained standing for many months until work commenced on its demolition – even the famous twin towers were not spared – before construction of the new stadium by the Australian contractor Multiplex started. This view, taken in 2003, shows the site cleared and initial work on the construction of the new ground.

16 June 2003
(695980)

► **A** year later, whilst still a building site, there is greater evidence that a new stadium was rising from the site. In particular, the dramatic arch, undoubtedly the defining symbol of the new Wembley, had been raised.

15 June 2004
(697411)

Further delays meant that the ground slipped bound its anticipated completion date of the end of the 2005/06 season and it looks likely as though the new ground will only open during the course of the 2006/07 season.

25 May 2006
(700271)

BARKING

The history of football in Barking is complex; suffice it here to note that a football club has been based in the borough since 1880 and from 1884 football was played at Vicarage Road, the ground illustrated in this view taken in the early 1960s. The club was known as Barking Institutes until 1902, Barking from 1902 until 1919 and again from 1932 until it merged in 2001 to become Barking & East Ham United, and Barking Town from 1919 until 1932. The ground as illustrated here, shortly after the installation of floodlights in 1958, was to be the home of the club until 1973 when the ground was acquired by the local council and the club leased a new ground in Mayesbrook Park.

7 July 1964
(A132824)

DAGENHAM & REDBRIDGE

The current occupants of Victoria Road — called the Glyn Hopkin Stadium following a three-year sponsorship deal signed in 2003 — are Dagenham & Redbridge, a team currently playing in the Nationwide Conference that came close to promotion to the Football League a couple of years ago. The club was formed in 1992 by the merger of the Dagenham and Redbridge clubs. The major change since the early 1980s are the new Carling (South) Stand and adjacent Barking College Family Stand; these were completed and refurbished respectively in 2002 and the ground's current capacity is just over 6,000, of which just over 1,000 can be seated.

26 June 2002
(693296)

DULWICH HAMLET

Dulwich Hamlet was established as a football club in 1893 and moved to Champion Hill in 1912. In its time Champion Hill was one of the most important non-league grounds in the country, used for Amateur Cup finals and other major fixtures. The ground as illustrated here shortly after the end of World War 2 was at its apogee, regularly attracting five-figure gates to a ground with a nominal capacity of 30,000. The ground as recorded here in this view looking towards the north was largely the result of major investment between 1929 and the opening of the rebuilt ground by Sir Frederick Wall, the then secretary of the FA, in October 1931. The facilities at the ground now included a covered enclosure for 2,000 fans and a covered stand accommodating 2,400. During the 1930s further upgrading work was undertaken, as the club reaped the financial rewards of its earlier investment. The ground remained largely unchanged until 1964 when a clubhouse was constructed and, in October of the same year, floodlighting was installed. However, by the early 1980s, the ground was increasingly careworn and, in conjunction with a superstore, the ground was rebuilt.

1949

(A22350/49)

ENFIELD

Southbury Road has been the home of Enfield since the club moved to the newly constructed ground in October 1936 having moved from the club's previous ground at Cherry Orchard Lane. The new ground, situated within the borough's playing fields, saw construction work start on 5 July 1936 and, by the time the ground opened on 31 October 1936, it was provided with a 120ft-long stand accommodating 750 on the west side and covered accommodation for a further 400 on the east; this is the condition of the ground viewed in this view taken towards the east in the early 1950s.

8 April 1954
(A53369/54)

◀ **T**he next phase in the development of the ground was the provision of a small cover at the north end of the ground; this view, taken in 1962 looking towards the south, shows this facility when brand new.

28 May 1962
(A100147)

▶ **I**n 1962, shortly after the date of the previous illustration, floodlighting was installed at the ground. Subsequently a short cover was installed at the south end of the ground, in this view looking towards the north in the early 1970s. Since the date of this photograph, the floodlighting has been replaced and more terracing installed.

10 February 1972
(A95247)

FINCHLEY

Although Finchley FC was founded in 1874 and had a number of grounds between then and the mid-1920s, it was not until 1929, when the club was promoted back to the Athenian League, that work started on Summers Lane. The Main Stand, on the east of the ground, was opened on 20 December 1930 and was provided with 600 seats. The following year, the stand was converted into a double-sided structure to provide accommodation for spectators watching rugby on the adjacent pitch. The ground itself saw its first game of football in 1932. Apart from the stand, the ground was provided with terracing and, in 1962, with floodlights for the first time. The original Finchley club merged with Wingate FC (a club founded in 1946 and named after Major General Orde Wingate) in 1991 to form Wingate & Finchley FC. As a result of the loss of its own ground in 1972, Wingate had in fact played for a period at Summers Lane in the mid-1970s (although the ground-sharing had not been a success). The reasoning behind the merger was that Wingate FC was well funded and Finchley was higher up the non-league structure and so, as a result, Wingate's funds and Finchley's status would lead to a successful and ambitious team. As a result of the merger, considerable investment has gone into the development of Summers Lane — or the Harry Abrahams Stadium as it is now known. Work included moving the pitch closer to the Main Stand and new floodlighting.

1982
(431535)

HAYES

Hayes – or Botwell Mission as the club was known until 1924 – moved into Church Road in 1920. The ground was provided with a Main Stand in 1925. The ground's clubhouse was destroyed by a bomb in 1942. The ground as illustrated in this view dating from the early 1960s shows the 450-seat brick built Main Stand with the covered terrace opposite providing accommodation for 1,000.

The original grass embankments were converted to open terraces in the years after World War 2. Some 40 years after the date of this photograph, the ground remains largely unchanged.

1 June 1963
(A112556)

HENDON

Hendon FC was founded as Christ Church Hampstead in 1908, becoming Hampstead Town in 1909 and plain Hampstead when the club moved to Claremont Road in 1926. In 1932 the club became Golders Green before adopting its current title in 1946. Work started on the construction of the new ground in June of that year with the club moving in for the start of the 1926/27 season. The ground was provided with a Main Stand, reseated in 1993 with a capacity of 387. The pavilion from the club's previous ground, Avenue Road, was relocated to the new ground. The ground was also provided with a covered terrace opposite the Main Stand and the grass banking was eventually fitted with concrete terracing. This view, taken in the mid-1960s, records the ground shortly after the installation of floodlighting in 1962; this was upgraded using the original pylons in 1971. The ground as recorded here is substantially the same as today, although the future of the club at Claremont Road is in serious doubt; the condition of the ground is poor with the Main Stand already condemned. The gate receipts are inadequate to fund the club and survival is by no means certain. The club have plans to relocate to the Copthall Stadium but this can only be achieved if the existing ground is redeveloped. As with a number of other grounds, however, there are covenants which prevent this and fans are campaigning to persuade Barnet Council, in whose area Hendon is based, to relax these.

26 November 1965
(A155711)

HORNCHURCH

The Stadium, Bridge Avenue, the home of AFC Hornchurch, was built by the local council on the site of a rubbish dump in 1952. Upminster Wanderers, as the club was initially known, was founded in 1923 and changed their name in 1953, on moving to the Stadium, to Hornchurch & Upminster, before becoming Hornchurch in 1961. The original Hornchurch FC collapsed as a result of financial problems and the new club was established to take over for the start of the 2005/06 season. The ground is provided with two stands – the Riverside (named after the adjacent River Ingrebourne) and the East –

and is also home to Havering Athletics Club. The ground illustrated here is as it existed in the early 1960s; in 1989 the clubhouse was destroyed by fire and, during the 2002/03 season the ground was substantially upgraded with new seats in the stands as a result of new financial backers who had ambitious plans to rebuild the ground as a football-only arena and relocate the athletics track. The financial collapse, however, prevented these plans being put into place.

1 August 1962
(A105934)

KINGSTONIAN

Richmond Road, illustrated here, was the home of Kingstonian until the club relocated to the new Kingsmeadow Stadium for the start of the 1989/90 season. The old ground was the third site used by the club along Richmond Road and was in fact the adjacent field to the second ground (which the club lost to Leyland Motors in 1920 as a result of rumours that the football club had folded). This view, taken looking towards the north, shows the Main Stand, built of wood in 1922, on the south side of the ground with the short western extension added in 1926; this structure was acquired second-hand from a local horse society. The ground was originally provided with banking but this was converted to concrete terracing after World War 2 and a covered enclosure was built on the north side of the ground opposite the Main Stand. the final development at Richmond Road came with the installation of floodlighting in the early 1960s. With the value of the land rocketing, the club elected to relocate to a new ground built on the site of the Norbiton Road Sports Ground; however, since relocation, the club's finances have deteriorated with the result that the main occupant of Kingsmeadow are AFC Wimbledon (the breakaway club established with the move of Wimbledon from London to Milton Keynes).

6 June 1973
(SV4650)

LEYTONSTONE

The compact ground at Granleigh Road was home to Leytonstone for almost a century until 1986 when the club relocated to Green Pond Road, home of Walthamstow Avenue, where the teams were to merge to form Redbridge Forest along with Ilford. This club was ultimately to merge with Dagenham to form Dagenham & Redbridge. The club was formed in 1886 and moved to Cranleigh Road eight years later. This view, taken towards the north, shows how confined the ground was. Bounded on the north side by the railway line, with Leytonstone High Road adjacent, the gardens of the adjacent terrace housing also restricted the ground. However, despite the constrictions, the club's record attendance at Granleigh Road was 10,500 achieved against Newport County during an FA Cup in 1951. Following the final game at the ground in April 1986, the site was cleared and used for housing.

24 November 1965
(A155467)

SOUTHALL

Southall FC's Western Road ground was one of the largest in non-league football and once accommodated almost 20,000 fans for an FA Cup tie against Watford in 1936. The football club's origins dated back to 1871, making it one of the oldest non-league teams in the country for many years. However, the origins of Western Road, viewed here in the early 1960s, are more uncertain. Whilst the early years of the ground are obscure, much of the development of the ground took place in the interwar years after the club's merger with Park Royal. It was during this period that the first grandstand – later destroyed by fire and a new stand built on the opposite side – was built as were the concrete terraces. Although a successful non-league team, with countless honours to its name (and several well-known players emerging from it), Southall's fortunes declined and, in the mid-1990s, is was forced to leave Western Road. Thereafter the club has had a somewhat nomadic existence, most recently ground-sharing at Yeading. Following the club's departure, Western Road gradually deteriorated until it was demolished and redeveloped for affordable housing in the late 1990s.

15 August 1963
(A118428)

WALTHAMSTOW

Walthamstow Avenue's origins dated back to a school team in the late 19th century adopting the name Walthamstow Avenue in 1903. The club was given land, previously used as allotments, in Green Pond in 1920 and work started after an appeal for funds on the construction of the new ground. The ground, when opened on 21 December 1921, included a wooden stand with clubhouse. During the 1920s and 1930s, open terracing was constructed. However, in 1938 fire destroyed the existing stand; a replacement, accommodating 1,000, was constructed, being opened on 26 August 1939. During the 1950s, covered accommodation was provided opposite the Main Stand and at the West End.

This is the condition recorded in this view of the ground taken in the early 1970s. A cover was subsequently added at the East End. In 1988 Walthamstow Avenue was taken over by Leytonstone/Ilford to form Redbridge Forest, a precursor of Dagenham & Redbridge. The new club, however, was not to remain at Green Pond Road for long as the club subsequently relocated to Dagenham's Victoria Road ground, ultimately to become Dagenham & Redbridge in 1992. Green Pond Road was subsequently demolished and the site used for housing.

13 July 1972
(A233872)

WELLING

Now the home of Welling United and of Erith & Belvedere FC, football was first played at Park View Road some 80 years ago. Prior to the outbreak of World War 2 the ground was provided with a grandstand but this suffered damage during the war and was subsequently demolished. After the war, Bexleyheath & Welling FC was reformed and work to revitalise Park View Road commenced. Initially, facilities were limited but in the 1950s a new Main Stand was constructed. This was extended and a cover installed over the opposite side, as shown in this view taken in the early 1960s, as the club's ambitions grew. In 1976, Bexley United, as the club was now known,

collapsed and Welling United became tenants of the ground with a 15-year lease. Work was required to enable the club to play at the ground, including work to repair fire damage in the Main Stand, before the first Welling home game on 26 August 1977. Welling United were joined at Park View Road in 1999 by Erith & Belvedere and, since that date, much work has been undertaken at the ground in order to improve facilities. This work has included the construction of a new stand on the Erith side (opposite the Main Stand).

16 May 1963
(A111719)